Taste and See
Savoring the Child's Wisdom

Pam Moore

**Catechesis of
the Good Shepherd
Publications**

TASTE AND SEE: SAVORING THE CHILD'S WISDOM © 2011 Archdiocese of Chicago: Liturgy Training Publications, 3949 South Racine Avenue, Chicago IL 60609; 1-800-933-1800; fax 1-800-933-7094; e-mail orders@ltp.org. All rights reserved. See our Web site at www.LTP.org.

Cover art by Vicky, age 8, of the True Vine Atrium of St. Matthew's Episcopal Church, Evanston IL. After creating this piece of artwork, Vicky said, "This is someone who loves the cross so much she carries it with her always." Art p. vii by Olivia, age 7, St. Matthew's Episcopal Church, Evanston IL. Art p. 8 by Adam, age 7, St. Charles's Episcopal Church, St. Charles IL. Art p. 65 by Lisa, age 10, St. Charles's Episcopal Church, St. Charles IL. Efforts were made to reach the creator of the art on p. 27, but the artist could not be located.

Printed in the United States of America.

Library of Congress Control Number: 2011929602

ISBN 978-1-61671-045-3

TSCW

CONTENTS

Introduction	Mrs. Moore, the Lord is with You	vi
Chapter 1	Nose to Nose with God	I
Chapter 2	Prayer in the Atrium	5
Chapter 3	God's Good Things	7
Chapter 4	Anger Going Down, Down	II
Chapter 5	A Good Man	I5
Chapter 6	Full of Joy	I9
Chapter 7	I Am in God	25
Chapter 8	I Hope My Birthday Comes Soon	29
Chapter 9	I Will Give My Soul and Life to the Lord	3I
Chapter 10	Naming the Atria	35
Chapter 11	Like a Kiss from God	39
Chapter 12	Your Enemies Are Like the Stars	45
Chapter 13	The Presents of God	5I
Chapter 14	The Gifts of God for the People of God	55
Chapter 15	Can We Read More?	59
Chapter 16	We Look Like God	63
Chapter 17	A Child's Icon of Unity	65
Chapter 18	My Favorite Part	7I
Chapter 19	The Empty Tomb	73
Chapter 20	A Serious Love	77
Chapter 21	A Tender Caress	8I
Bibliography		85

To the children of St. Matthew's Church in Evanston, IL
and St. Charles's Church in St. Charles, IL

Your inner reflections guide us, never imposing anything on us or telling us how to feel or think. They are actually as radical as the purpose statement of the Catechesis. When you spoke about "creating time and space for children and God to interact," and then just mentioned that "it requires setting aside one's own hopes and aspirations," I stopped breathing. It's true, it's what Jesus said, but it's one of those "hard sayings."

—Valentina "Tina" Lillig, 1945–2009,
after reading an early draft of the book

Mrs. Moore, the Lord is with You

When I first started working in an atrium of the Catechesis of the Good Shepherd in 1989 and soon after became the Director of Children's Formation at my church, I often found slips of paper left in the atrium or tucked under my office door or slipped into my hand at the end of an atrium session. They all said, "Mrs. Moore, the Lord is with you." At first I would read them, smile contentedly at the children's growing sense of God which I was proudly providing, and then toss them in the nearest waste paper basket. After a few years the notes barely trickled in. Now I wish I had saved some of them. I look back at those notes and wonder if the children were trying to tell me not to worry. God is in this work. I don't need to work so hard trying to make it perfect. I noticed that the children's notes always spoke in the present tense: "The Lord *is* with you," rather than the usual call to prayer, "The Lord *be* with you," with the familiar response, "And also with you" / "And with your spirit." Like the angel's announcement to Mary, the children named a present reality, an ongoing relationship: "Greetings, favored one! The Lord is with you . . . . Do not be afraid" (Luke 1:28–30).

Now, twenty plus years later, I can see that those first children knew exactly what they were talking about. God has been with me.

Jesus the Good Shepherd has led me to many green pastures filled with innumerable people with whom I have had the privilege of sharing this incredible work. Most of all, I now know that the children themselves have been and continue to be the Lord who is with me. The children have shown me, taught me, and waited for me to recognize them as the voice of God calling me into a more authentic and peaceful relationship with the Good Shepherd. Like a prophet, the child has a word for the adult world. It is a candid word of healing and hope as well as utter delight in the One who knows us each by name and leads us to our hearts' desire. I know I am not alone when I say these things.

Our vocation as catechists is a gift and a mystery—a precious pearl which gives us unbounded joy, a hidden treasure for which we willingly purchase the whole field, the leaven which lifts and enriches every aspect of our lives, and a seed gradually growing, maturing, becoming something more exquisite moment by moment; "[we] do not know how" (Mark 4:27b). It seems to me, then, that integral to this Catechesis as the meeting place of two mysteries— the mystery of God and the mystery of the child—is the mystery of the conversion of the adult by the child. In fact, that is what this entire book is about. It is, as the title indicates, about savoring the wisdom of the child precisely because we catechists are engaged in the mysterious process of growth and transformation. I don't think any of us works in an atrium only for the children. We find the atrium experience feeds our souls as well, and it does so in ways we can barely believe or name.

We have all had at least a few experiences with children in our atria that have caught our attention because a child's artwork, comment, or prayer was so unusual, profound, or perfectly essential. Over the years, I have used these experiences to communicate the key points of the Catechesis of the Good Shepherd to parents and the whole parish via monthly newsletters. In fact, I write constantly because, by doing so, I can think more deeply and concretely about the child's way of knowing and living close to God in Christ the Good Shepherd. These periods of reflection in turn help me draw closer to God myself. I am not saying anything new when I say the children have led me to a completely new relationship with the living God. This is what Maria Montessori, Sofia Cavalletti, Gianna Gobbi, and their collaborators have been saying for decades—not to mention Jesus' sayings about the children. The child is our teacher. The youngest and least likely among us possesses divine wisdom. All we need do is watch them and listen to them. This brings us to the ongoing task of observing children within and beyond our atria and to the purpose of this book.

I gathered my newsletter articles together into this collection in order to offer other catechists an additional way to continue observing, pondering, and being transformed by the child's spontaneous artistic and verbal proclamations. In other words, *Taste and See: Savoring the Child's Wisdom* is an invitation to further formation in this Catechesis. While our formation courses are essential and any additional study of Scripture, liturgy, or the Montessori method is beneficial, the child remains our first and primary source of knowledge, understanding, joy, and conversion. This book is about hearing, naming, and really chewing on those verbal and non-verbal responses.

Like feasting at a grand banquet, enjoying every morsel and moment, marveling at the chef's artistry, and wanting it to go on forever, savoring the child's uncanny wisdom evokes the psalmist's song: "O taste and see that the Lord is good" (Psalm 34:8a). I also see savoring the child's wisdom as a gentler, less arduous angle on our task of observing the child. Savoring implies prolonged admiration and continual rumination. When we savor something, we take the experience with us, cherishing the initial moment of delight well into the future.

I also think the phrase "savoring the child's wisdom" corresponds to and supports the maturity of the Catechesis of the Good Shepherd and its catechists today. Throughout the years, we have been compelled to spread the word about this amazing approach to children's religious formation. Now it is time to pause in our excitement and consider in gratitude, in wonder, and in openness to even greater transformation the many ways in which the child leads us to new understanding and experiences of divine life and love.

This invitation to savor the child's wisdom comes at a time in the history of the National Association of the Catechesis of the Good Shepherd when many practical organizational issues demand attention. Even as we attend to these necessary concerns, we remember that the primary focus of our work is the child. The child anchors us in humility and asks only for satisfying food: the Gospel and the signs of the sacraments.

My hope is that the following reflections will provide the pause we need from time to time, and especially at this moment in our collective life together. It doesn't really matter in what order you read the chapters. Just choose one to savor for a week, month, or season. If you do choose to read them from the beginning, you may notice that I organized them such that the earliest ones focus on the most concrete components of atrium life. Later chapters have more theological content and ruminations. I also hope you will use these reflections as springboards for meditating on the wisdom you glean from the children in your atrium. I highly recommend keeping a journal of your experiences with the children. You might start your journal while reading these reflections, noting similarities from your own experiences or aspects of the Catechesis of the Good Shepherd, the Gospel, or the sacraments to which you want to pay particular attention while observing your children. We've included some of the children's artwork for your meditation. You may also consider meditating on a child's drawing or art or reflecting on a child's prayer or response, perhaps re-creating them in some way.

Someday, I hope to embroider the child's drawing of God's "yes" or make an illustration of the child's maxim: "Your enemies are like the stars in the sky. You should love them." What a treat it would be to travel the country photographing people making atrium materials. These photos could accompany the child's statement after hearing about the man who made the sheepfold for the parable of the Good Shepherd presentation: "He must be a good man." The possibilities for savoring the child's wisdom are endless. Through it all, there is just one thing to remember, "The Lord is with you."

CHAPTER ONE

Nose to Nose with God

One day I asked the children what comes to mind when they think of communion. One child said, "You and me and me and you." Another said, "Friendship." Others said, "Food, eating, eating together." "Bread and wine." "The great thanksgiving." The last child said, "It's being nose to nose with God."

With few words, little effort, and much confidence, this last child names the heart of living in relationship with God. This child's response, however, did not convey the confrontational or competitive "nose to nose" forceful spirit that often dominates society, but the mutual delight of being in the presence of another whose love we know and trust completely. This is why we say that in the atrium we listen to God with children. When we are attentive to children, that is, when we are "nose to nose" with them, we see that they take us right to the core truths of the Christian faith. Even though adults are the ones who make the initial proclamation, children get right to what is most essential. The result is mutual blessing. Therefore, the aim of the Catechesis of the Good Shepherd is twofold—to initiate children into the Christian life and faith and to initiate the Church into the ways children reveal new nuances of our shared life with God in Christ.

Jesus points to this mutuality when he put a child in the midst of the disciples' argument about who is the greatest (see Matthew 18:1–3, Mark 9:33–36, Luke 9:46–48) and, in effect, says you must pay attention to children, or otherwise, you will miss out on a significant perspective of the kingdom of God. More precisely, you must assume the role of the servant, living nose to nose with the littlest among you, for "whoever wants to be first, must be last of all and servant of all" (Mark 9:35). Jesus points to himself as model, saying, "I came not to be served but to serve" (Matthew 20:28, Mark 10:45).

Therefore, catechists of the Montessori-based Catechesis of the Good Shepherd believe children are already living in relationship with God, the Holy Spirit is the only real teacher, and adults prepare a sacred space called the atrium so that each child can encounter the love of God in his or her own way and at his or her own rhythm. In short, we strive to satisfy the child's silent plea: "Help me come closer to God myself."[1]

From this perspective, serving the child's religious life rather than teaching Bible stories, definitions, and creeds is the Church's primary function. This does not mean we are not concerned that children know the stories and tenets of the faith, only that we strive to discern and place the religious needs and capabilities of the child before our own desire to measure the results of our efforts. We strive to remember that "nothing belongs to the adult, neither what she or he transmits, nor the soul of the child; they belong to God."[2] Hebrew scholar Sofia Cavalletti, who developed this catechesis along with Montessorian Gianna Gobbi, explains: "The help the adult can give the child is only preliminary and peripheral and one that halts—that must halt—on the threshold of the 'place' where God speaks with His creature."[3] What this catechesis offers children is not merely instruction, but a service, one that acknowledges and supports the seed of faith that is the birthright of every human being.

With the goal being one of assisting the child in his or her growing faith, this catechesis is better understood as offering a service of pastoral care or spiritual direction to children. As such, the main task of the catechist, like that of the spiritual director, is one of listening. Listening means being *nose to nose* with the child and involves preparing the atrium with sensorial materials from all the areas in which human beings experience God: Scripture, liturgy, and daily life. It also involves observing the children's use of the materials as well as their artwork and verbal responses. Like the well-trained spiritual director, the catechist does not impose his or her own views or interpretations, but listens and observes as the child slowly reveals his or her experience and knowledge of God and gently directs the child to other divine treasures as they have been kept for us in the Bible and as we live in liturgy.

In the process of listening to children in the atrium, catechists are often graced with startling new ways of describing, encountering, pondering, and living their own lives with Jesus the Good Shepherd, who calls each by name so that "they may have life and have it to the full" (John 10:10b). Therefore, while serving the unique religious needs and capacities of children, this Catechesis transforms adults and the whole Church as well. Its main purpose, as stated in the purpose statement of the National Association of the Catechesis of the Good Shepherd, is "to assist in the involvement of adults and children in a common religious experience in which the religious values of childhood predominate."

How radical it is to claim to assist children, as well as the accompanying adults, rather than to teach, offer, provide, promote, facilitate, initiate, create, mold, or implement a curriculum! Assisting another requires being *nose to nose* with them, waiting, watching, and gradually discovering what they need rather than depositing what we want them to have, know, or become. How easy it is for a catechist to forget that being a matchmaker between the child and God is the primary role of the adult. Selecting the images of God, Scripture texts, liturgical signs and symbols, and corresponding tangible materials that correspond to children's unique religious nature takes a lifetime of attention, as evidenced by Sofia Cavalletti, Gianna Gobbi, and their collaborators who developed the Catechesis of the Good Shepherd over a period of sixty plus years in Rome, Italy. Cavalletti is still modifying it according to her ongoing observation of children's interactions with the catechetical materials.

Creating time and space for children and God to meet sounds simple, but it is not. It requires setting aside one's own hopes and aspirations, time frames, and goals and becoming the unprofitable servant who expects no thanks because "we have only done what we ought to have done!" (Luke 17:10). We proclaim the Gospel then step back and let the Holy Spirit direct each child toward the atrium material that satisfies and sustains his or her religious life. Most often children choose something we would never have imagined. This is where relinquishing our preconceived ideas about what children need smacks us in the face. In these moments, we must ask ourselves: "Do I trust that God is working in the child?" "Do I trust that God and the child are nose to nose?"

---

1. See the cover of the Catechesis of the Good Shepherd Blue Brochure available from the National Office of the Catechesis of the Good Shepherd, P.O. Box 1084, Oak Park, IL 60304.

2. Sofia Cavalletti quoted by Gianna Gobbi in "The Meaning, Importance and Limitations of Our Catechetical Materials," *Journals of the Catechesis of the Good Shepherd 1998–2002* (Chicago: Liturgy Training Publications, 2003): 105.

3. Sofia Cavalletti, *The Religious Potential of the Child* (Chicago: Liturgy Training Publications, 1992): 52.

CHAPTER TWO

Prayer in the Atrium

A catechist calls a child by name and invites him to place the white marble statue of Jesus the Good Shepherd in the center of a small table. She invites another to place a candle; another places the Bible. Others bring vases of flowers or a card with a short Scripture verse. When all have had a turn and the table, which is called a prayer table, is completely adorned, all eyes rest on its beauty, bodies still and voices quiet. It is time for prayer. However, this formal gathering for communal prayer is not the only time prayer occurs in the atrium. It simply marks the end of a whole morning of prayerful activity in the atrium.

That is to say, the atrium reflects Saint Benedict's premise that the pots and pans in the kitchen possess the same potential for conversation with God as do the articles of the altar. It is a place where the activities of daily life and those pertaining to Scripture and liturgy are given the same dignity. In short, the atrium is a place where working with the catechetical materials becomes conversation with God. The holy and the ordinary rest side by side and the children move freely between them. The Montessori exercises of pouring beans from one pitcher to another, arranging flowers in glass vases, dusting the shelves, and drawing, as well as the atrium work of copying Scripture, setting the model altar, reenacting the parable of the Good Shepherd by moving the two-dimensional, wooden figures of sheep and shepherd, all culti-vate attentiveness and reverence for every aspect of life.

This is life in the atrium. The aim is not so much religious instruction as religious life. In the Preface to Sofia Cavalletti's *The Religious Potential of the Child*, Mark Searle reminds us that "too often religious education is so goal-oriented and curriculum-conscious that it loses sight of its mission to minister to the religious life of the child."[1] This is the aim of the Catechesis of the Good Shepherd—to be attentive to children's unique religious needs and capabilities. Acting as matchmakers between God and the child, we offer an education to prayer; that is, we offer opportunities for children to make their own responses before introducing specific prayers trea-sured by the Church for generations.

One spring day, eight-year-old Alice showed me just how readily children form their own conversation with God. I turned my head just in time to see her slip a piece of paper out the win-dow of our second floor atrium. When I asked her what that was all about, she responded casually, "Oh, I write letters to God all the time and send them right off."

In the end, the formal prayer time as well as the individual work-response time becomes a process whereby children and adults name for each other the abundant life of God that is pres-ent in the midst of all of life.

---

1. Sofia Cavalletti, *The Religious Potential of the Child* (Chicago: Liturgy Training Publications, 1992): 4.

CHAPTER THREE

God's Good Things

A favorite work of some children in the atrium is the tracing cards with drawings of the objects of the altar, the kingdom parables, and the stories surrounding the birth of Jesus. Sometimes the children will assemble all their tracings into a booklet with the colored paper provided for covers. When I first started working in an atrium, a six-year-old titled her booklet of the objects of the altar: "God's Good Things." The next year another child put her tracings of the infancy narratives together, writing on the cover: "Come Let Us Gather." After Christmas of that same year a seven-year-old boy pasted Christmas cards on paper, writing short descriptions of what was happening in each scene. For Jesus' birth he wrote: "Jesus was there giggling away."

The joy these children exude is the hallmark of the religious life, the sign under which the Catechesis of the Good Shepherd was born, and one of the religious values implied in this Catechesis's purpose statement. It is not a giddy, depleting, birthday party kind of joy, but the serene joy that emerges from an inner stability that is rooted in something other than one's self—a deeply felt relationship with the Giver of Life. It is the joy that comes from knowing everything is a gift from God. Even these young children know the chalice and paten as well as the altar cloth, cruets, corporal, and candles, are more than utilitarian. They are not merely objects, but signs of the gift of God given to us in Jesus our Good Shepherd. They are indeed God's good things. They are the incarnation of

And Mary was laying down and holding Jeus

Josepl just was as hap y as Mary.

Jeus was there gigling away.

the sheapards Just stood there looking at the lord

God's desire to remain with all humanity for all eternity. The incarnation of God's love for us through the Eucharistic feast begins with the mystery of the Incarnation, of God becoming human in the person of Jesus who invites all to come and gather around and watch as divine life delights in assuming human form so much so that this divine child lies there giggling away. Could it be that these children give a perspective of the Incarnation that even the Gospels neglect to convey—the perspective of the child Jesus? Matthew and Luke's accounts of the birth of Jesus are written with an eye on adult activities—traveling, registering, finding a place to stay, listening to the angels, and following the star. Saying Jesus lay there giggling away communicates a different vantage point—that of the child enjoying life.

The religious potential of the child of which Sofia Cavalletti speaks in her books by the same name pertains not only to what children might become as a result of careful attention to their religious needs and capabilities, but also to recognizing the unique perspective of the child. Children unselfconsciously proclaim new nuances of the Word of God, and these have the potential for transforming adult hearts and minds. If that is the case, then perhaps the doctrinal content that Catechesis of the Good Shepherd catechists are required to name for each atrium presentation should include the child's perspective. In the case of the stories pertaining to the birth of Jesus, the doctrine might read something like: God's continuing love and presence with all people as spoken of by the prophets becomes concrete in Emmanuel, God-with-us, who lays there giggling away as we gather 'round. Or, Jesus is truly God and truly human and lays there giggling away: come let us gather. Or, he who exists for all eternity initiates his human story in a specific place and at a particular moment and lays there giggling away, coaxing us to gather near him full of similar childlike joy and wonder.

CHAPTER FOUR

Anger Going Down, Down

It was the second Sunday of Advent, and a group of six to eight-year-old children and I were gathered in the atrium. We lit two candles on the Advent wreath, and then began reading the prophecy of preparing the way from Isaiah 40:3–5:

A voice cries out:
"In the wilderness prepare the way of the LORD,
   make straight in the desert a highway for our God.
Every valley shall be lifted up,
and every mountain and hill be made low;
the uneven ground shall become level,
   and the rough places a plain.
Then the glory of the Lord shall be revealed,
   and all people shall see it together,
   for the mouth of the LORD has spoken."

I asked the children what they thought was being made low and what was being lifted up. I barely had the question out of my mouth when one child said, "It's like the anger going down, down, and the happiness and goodness are being lifted up." A second child continued, "The anger gets buried and covered over and goodness is planted in its place and it grows like a flower."

How many times have I heard this passage read at the beginning of Advent or Lent, nodded my head knowingly, and then went on to something else? How many times have I thought of it as a nice saying, but never really took it seriously, felt its power, or really imagined what it could mean? This is such a familiar text. All of the accounts of the Gospel have it. It's John the Baptist's famous proclamation, yet who has unlocked its riches like these children? How often has this text been presented only as an invitation to change ourselves, do our own preparing, clean up our own clutter, and purify our own hearts rather than as an announcement of God's plan to bring forth a new heaven and a new earth? How often are biblical texts turned into moral imperatives, forgetting or ignoring the divine love that propels human thought and human history? How often do Christian education curricula turn in the same direction?

These children's responses point us toward the divine presence hidden within the human desire for justice and peace. They reveal both the depth of the text at hand and children's ability to penetrate Scripture. There is so much more to be discovered and honored in both. When invited into conversation, children exhibit a keen ability to recognize and name the truth. They show the rest of us that this familiar text is not merely about changing human behavior, but about God's plan to make all things new. Notice that they do not say, as adults are prone to say, "We must put our anger aside. We must work out our differences, arrogance, greed, and so on," or, "We must do good works. We must help the flowers of goodness bloom. We must build up the community through patient love. We must serve others' needs." Instead, the children quickly perceive that the divine plan for the decrease of anger and the increase of goodness takes precedence over human action. Children do not jump in and try to fix things or impose their ideas of how to make the world a better place. Instead, they recognize and pause in wonder at the announcement of divine life and love as it animates human history. They remind us that the hope for peace and harmony among people; the desire for the end of anger, violence, and war; and the welling up of goodness are not human inventions, but divine ones.

Children remind us that announcements of the in-breaking of the kingdom of God always come as gift in the form of parable, image, or story for our prolonged meditation. Like Jesus, the first child begins with the suggestion: "It's like . . . ." By offering a comparison, children, like Jesus, give us concrete images to ponder and savor. The second child paints an even more vivid picture: "Anger gets buried and covered over and goodness is planted in its place and it grows like a flower." The growing parables of the kingdom paint similar scenes: tiny mustard seeds grow steadily until one day there's a shrub so large many birds build nests in its branches; and a small amount of leaven mixed into a large batch of flour and water eventually lifts the dough to a robust loaf of bread that can be shared with many.

By lifting up the divine perspective of what "shall be," children direct our attention toward the divine hope that human beings will have eyes to see and ears to hear the innumerable ways in which God inspires both adults and children to be heralds of God's reign on earth. Neither child nor adult possesses complete understanding, but together, the truth of the kingdom of God becomes clear and the ability to adapt ourselves to it smoother. The mountains of anger that will be made low and the valleys of goodness that will be lifted up require divine and human participation. Children assist adults in recognizing the divine spark permeating all, and adults assist children by creating an environment in which each child can recognize and express the knowledge of God within himself or herself. In so doing, the anxiety about children learning and living the Christian life and faith is made low and the awareness of children's religious capacities is lifted up. When this becomes a full reality, "the glory of the Lord shall, indeed, be revealed."

(An earlier version of this essay was published in *The Catechesis of the Good Shepherd Journal* 24 [2009]: 28–29.)

CHAPTER FIVE

A Good Man

After presenting the parable of the Good Shepherd in the Catechesis of the Good Shepherd fashion to my group of four-year-olds in the Lutheran preschool where I spend my week days, one little boy asked, "Who made this?" When I told him a man from my church made the wooden figures of Shepherd, sheep, and sheepfold, he responded softly, "He must be a good man."

How interesting that a child outside the atrium senses the inherent beauty of well-crafted, wooden items as well as the devotion of its maker. In this Catechesis, we strive to gather and construct the atrium materials from natural sources like wood, glass, pottery, wicker, brass, fabric, fresh flowers, living plants, and prints of fine art. Since the Word we proclaim is the most precious Word of all, the materials are built to incarnate and reflect that same precious quality. This child shows us the difference it makes. His comment—"He must be a good man"—reminds me how sensitive children are to their surroundings. They absorb everything in a holistic way, with body, mind, and soul. This child's body had quieted, his mind was attentive, and his soul seemed satisfied. The proclamation of the parable of the Good Shepherd with the wooden figures touched him deeply, so much so that he wanted to know who created them. He knew the creator/Creator must be good to have made something so beautiful for him. Beautifully made materials—maps of Israel, dioramas of the life of Christ, models of the altar and baptismal font—reveal the maker's devotion to Jesus. In fact, making the atrium materials is a way for adults to absorb the Word more deeply—to absorb it as children do, into our very bodies. It is especially helpful for visual and kinetic learners. Material-making slows us down, helping us "to combat hurry, consumerism and even excessive 'efficiency'. . . . [It helps us assume] the rhythm of the child and thus also—or so we believe. . . the working of the Holy Spirit."[1] After ten years in this work, I decided to try my hand at making wooden figures, so I purchased a jig saw and started cutting out these same figures of shepherd and sheep. It was only then that I realized that no two sheep are alike, and that is part of the beauty and gift of making the atrium materials. We are given an opportunity to enter the parable in a new way. Manipulating the birch plywood around the saw blade required great attention. In the process, I found new understanding of Jesus' words, "I know my own and my own know me just as the Father knows me and I know the Father" (John 10: 14–15). I, too, know which sheep's ear is notched, which one's leg was nearly cut off, which one's nose is pointed. Our Good Shepherd knows the minutest details and defects of our being and loves us profusely anyway. We have indeed been "searched out and known":

> For it was you who formed my inward parts;
> you knit me together in my mother's womb.
> I praise you, for I am fearfully and wonderfully made.
> Wonderful are your works;
> that I know very well.
> My frame was not hidden from you,
> when I was being made in secret,
> intricately woven in the depths of the earth.
> (Psalm 139:13–15).

So, too, atrium materials are made in the secret places of catechists' hearts, minds, hands, and homes. New understanding comes to us through the work of our hands and from God who created us and calls us to this work of honoring children's religious lives. Ever so slowly, we penetrate the mystery of God in the child and become good men and women.

---

1. Sofia Cavalletti, *The Religious Potential of the Child 6-12 Years Old* (Chicago: Liturgy Training Publications, 2002): Appendix I, no. 25, p. 137.

CHAPTER SIX

Full of Joy

The atrium presentation that day was the Visitation of Mary to Elizabeth. The group of fifteen preschool age children gathered on the rug with their catechists. It was a small rug for so many children, but no one seemed to mind. Each wiggled his or her way in. Each was clearly eager to see and hear the proclamation that would soon be made. Though snuggled shoulder to shoulder, the children listened quietly as the catechist read the account from Luke 1:39–45 and then re-presented it with the wooden model of Elizabeth's house and clay figures of Mary and Elizabeth. When the catechist posed a few meditative questions, most of the children remained silent but attentive. A few responded. One question posed was: "I wonder what it means to be filled with the Holy Spirit?" This drew a particularly solemn silence, and then one child quietly suggested, "Maybe it means being full of joy, so much joy that you want to dance."

I wonder how it is that children see, hear, know, and name joy as the sign of the indwelling of the Holy Spirit. Perhaps the place to begin is in the children's constant eagerness to see and hear each presentation of Scripture or liturgy in the atrium. Without fail, they immediately draw near, elbowing one another and craning their necks to see and be as close as possible. At a recent Baptism, I was reminded that this behavior extends beyond the atrium walls. When the priest invited the children to come and sit near the font, they did so without hesitation. Children do this everywhere—in libraries, classrooms, science exhibits, grocery stores, kitchens, museums, and zoos. As I continue watching children exhibit a desire to be as close as possible, I wonder about this ability and need in them. I also wonder about the fact that the child who made the suggestion in the atrium that day did not get up and dance or become silly or rambunctious. The joy he hinted at seemed more inward, more like contentment, more like a precious gift.

Sofia Cavalletti has observed that when children encounter the love of God through Jesus the Good Shepherd, they exude a joy that calms rather than excites them. They appear peaceful and serene. She has concluded that joy indicates that a vital human need has been met. It is the same no matter what our age. Happiness and pleasurable experiences are fleeting and often depleting, but joy is restorative. It conveys the satisfaction of a deeply desired encounter. Unlike happiness or pleasure, which come from the outside and are associated with things, joy radiates from the inside out. It reveals an inner stability that is rooted in something other than one's self—a deeply felt relationship with the Giver of Life. With that comes a deeply felt connection to all of life. Though it calms, joy is an enormously compelling force, pushing a person beyond himself or herself. Even in the face of opposition, uncertainty, and even death, joy motivates. The lives of the saints, past and present, reveal the compelling force of joy. It replaces fear and anxiety precisely because it is other-directed.

The five-year-old who said being filled with the Holy Spirit is like being so full of joy that one might dance illustrates this outward movement. The "dance" that joy initiates is more than a little jig or fleeting eruption of spiritual ecstasy. Valuable as those activities are, the joy that sustains us for the long haul is more like an undercurrent that gives our life meaning and direction. It compels us to take on tasks we might not otherwise assume. It compels us because it is not from us but from the deep well of divine presence in us. It compels us to draw near, as children do, to that which gives life.

Those who are involved in the work of the Catechesis of the Good Shepherd know something of this joy and the resulting compulsion to "go and make disciples of all nations" (Matthew 28:19). We do it for ourselves as much as for the children. We do it because our vital need for relationship with the living God is met, renewed, and enriched. We do it because in it we know that we are called by name by Jesus the Good Shepherd and nothing thrills us more than being known by our Lord. As a result, we possess that irresistible urge to share the life we have found. Our passion often surprises us as well as those around us. As one such person myself, I have often wondered what it is that is so compelling. After years of deliberation, I have come to the conclusion that it is because the Catechesis of the Good Shepherd invites us into a relationship with God that is replete with dignity. That is, it acknowledges each person's—child and adult alike—capacity to discern for himself or herself the ways in which Jesus is calling him or her to abundant life and full joy. Children know, just as we knew as children, what is good and true and real. We know from childhood onward that "there is religion and then there is the Spirit."[1]

Like happiness, joy cannot be attained by conscious striving. It comes as an unexpected and unimaginable gift—like the urge to dance. Even if we are told ahead of time about the joy involved, we cannot imagine it or create it. Perhaps that is why the people I encourage to take the Catechesis of the Good Shepherd formation courses see only the enormous commitment involved. I cannot create the inner joy that comes from the Holy Spirit and sustains a catechist. It always comes as a surprise. It is the surprise and joy of discovering, as the psalmist knew, that God:

. . . [has] searched me out and known me (Psalm 139:1)

He drew me out of the desolate pit,
out of the miry bog,
and set my feet upon a rock . . .
He put a new song in my mouth,
a song of praise to our God (Psalm 40:2–3)

> I have a goodly heritage . . . .
> Therefore, my heart is glad (Psalm 16:5, 9)
>
> And I will praise the Lord as long as I live (Psalm 146:2a)
>
> For great is his steadfast love towards us (Psalm 119:16)
>
> O Lord, I am your servant (Psalm 116:16)
>
> Therefore, my heart is glad and my soul rejoices;
> my body also rests secure (Psalm 16:9)

The link between being known by name and joy, praise, gratitude, and servanthood is unmistakable in these Psalms. Those who live in joy cannot help but give themselves over to "the call to become what we were meant to become—the call to achieve our 'vital design' . . . and even this is not what we 'ought to do'; rather . . . we cannot do otherwise."[2] This is true surrender. In his careful study and deeply personal experience of discerning the essence of servant leadership, Joseph Jawarski speaks of the "integrity of surrender," saying that what we are surrendering to is "the unfolding of the universe,"[3] because "the organizing principle of the universe is 'relatedness,' . . . this is more fundamental than 'thingness.'"[4] He articulates, in secular terms, the essence of John's Gospel, especially in the parables of the Good Shepherd and the True Vine: "I am the Good Shepherd. I know my sheep and my sheep know me." And "I am the Vine and you are the branches. Abide in my love."

It is not surprising, then, that immediately following Jesus' proclamation, "I have said all this to you so that my joy may be in you and your joy may be complete" (John 15:11), he says, "love one another as I have loved you" (John 15:12). That is, love out of the joy that you have known as a result of being my sheep and being branches on my Vine. When that happens, we have indeed become his servants, yet his joy transforms servanthood: "I do not call you servants any longer, because the servant does not know what the master is doing, but I have called you friends, because

I have made known to you everything that I have heard from my Father" (John 15:15).

In the end, Jesus' statement rings with new understanding: "You did not choose me but I chose you. And I appointed you to go and bear fruit, fruit that will last, so that the Father will give you whatever you ask him in my name" (John 15:16). Servanthood, rather than being something we set out to accomplish or a burden we must bear, becomes a vocation rooted in a deeply felt joy, and therefore cannot be resisted because, like children sitting shoulder to shoulder in order to hear and see things in the atrium, we, too, crane our necks forward in order to hear again the voice that calls us by name and leads us out to full joy.

---

1. Robert Coles, *The Spiritual Life of Children* (Boston: Houghton and Mifflin Co., 1990): xviii.

2. Joseph Jawarski, *Synchronicity: The Inner Path of Leadership* (San Francisco: Berrett-Koehler, 1998): 119.

3. Ibid., 12.

4. Ibid., 57.

CHAPTER SEVEN

I Am in God

Periodically, the primary grade children are scheduled to be the oblation bearers in the Sunday Mass, bringing the gifts of bread and wine to the altar at the offertory. When I invited them to make or select something from the atrium to bring to the altar along with the bread and wine, they immediately set out creating an assortment of "gifts." They all knew precisely what they wanted to offer. There was no deliberation or hesitation. Instead they set right to work. Some even declared aloud, "I know what I'm making." Within minutes one child brought me an origami cup and excitedly proclaimed, "This is God and Jesus." Then peeking inside she drew out a much smaller cup, saying, "And this is me. I am in God."

Of course, I was stunned into silence. What adult would ever imagine bringing forward so beautiful an icon of his or her relationship with God? Who is even aware enough to think of depicting it in so eloquent a fashion? Who even comes to the Eucharist with so much self-giving and confidence? How many volumes on sacramental theology have been written, yet barely touch the beauty and joy of the Eucharistic experience this child knows and radiates?

It is sure evidence that the essential realities of our faith require a certain simplicity—the ability to uncover and name that which is most essential. This child named the essence of the Eucharist as a sacrament of unity and covenant, as the gift that binds us all together and to Christ, the Good Shepherd. In this child, the gift of Christ's life is given and fully received. Communion is a source of immense joy. In her joy, this child brings to her relationship with God "all the dignity of a true partner, of one who listens to the voice that calls him [her] and takes great delight in responding to it."[1] In her sign and in her proclamation, the paradox of humility becomes clear—"[t]he smaller we feel the greater our joy."[2] This child reminds me that humility emerges when we come face to face with the gift of God in the sacraments and in our daily lives. The smallness experienced in true humility is not a belittling, but a recognition and exultation of the grandeur of God. God's greatness does not diminish us, but rather lifts us up so that, as Mother Teresa used to say, we can "do small things extraordinarily well." In our smallness there is great potential. Like the mustard seed that eventually becomes a beautiful shrub in which all the birds of the air can shelter in the shade, we possess tremendous potential for extending our hearts, minds, hands, and lives to others and in doing so radiate the joy born within the cup of God.

It occurs to me that this child's humility as expressed in her gesture of placing her cup inside God's cup and then showing both to me mirrors the priest's gestures of epiclesis and doxology or offering. Placing her small cup inside the larger one mirrors the gesture of epiclesis when the priest slowly lowers his hands over the bread and wine, asking the Holy Spirit to sanctify these gifts. When the child lifted up the two cups, one inside the other, she demonstrated the gesture of doxology or offering when the priest lifts up the chalice and paten praying: "By Him, with Him, in Him, in the unity of the Holy Spirit all glory and honor are yours, Almighty Father, now and forever"[3] or "Through him, and with him, and in him, / O God, almighty Father, / in the unity of the Holy Spirit, / all glory and honor is yours, / for ever and ever."[4]

The Great Amen that follows the doxology/offering was depicted in another child's drawing of the altar with a large, decorated U-shape over it and the word *yes* written inside. The seven-year-old child said the U-shape was the tongue of God—God's "yes" to us. Our Amen, our "yes," originates in God. Just as the first child so eloquently illustrated and as so many two- and three-year-olds the world over have shown us with their drawings of two circles, one inside the other, saying the larger one is the Good Shepherd and the smaller one inside is the sheep, we are all in God.

Children seem to live in comfortable intimacy with God and eagerly incarnate that relationship in their artwork. Children get along well with God. Books of children's own prayers to God reveal their candid conversations with the One whom they know and trust completely. Our task as catechists, parents, and teachers is to watch and listen to children as they demonstrate, in the most astoundingly brief ways, their ongoing life within God. In his influential book *The Spiritual Life of Children*, Robert Coles makes this confession when his colleagues, particularly Anna Freud, suggested that he let the children he was interviewing teach him something about themselves:

> At the time I was rather put off—I thought she was telling me that close attention to boys and girls as they talked about religious issues would bring me closer to the way my own thinking, some

of it childish, made use of religious interests. But years later . . .
I realized she meant precisely what she said: she had in mind
no condescension or accusation of psychopathology—[this]
project . . . helped me see children as seekers, as young pilgrims
well aware that life is a finite journey and as anxious to make sense
of it as those of us who are farther along in the time allotted us.[5]

I wonder what the world and the Church would be like if more adults did precisely that? What would happen if adults incarnated or illustrated this great reality—this covenant between God and humanity—in some tangible way? What would happen if adults took children's religious lives as seriously as they take children's religious education? It's pretty obvious what happens when we don't. We tend to be like the disciples, anxiously asking, "Who is the greatest?" Translated: "What's the best program?" "What must the Church do to get and keep families in the Church?" "What atrium materials do I need to make for Sunday?" Perhaps Jesus responded to this perennial adult question by putting a child in their midst and saying, "Unless you change and become like children, you will never enter the kingdom of heaven" (Matthew 18:3) because only children recognize the greatness of God as the gift that it is. Only children pay attention to God rather than a program. Unless we are able to see ourselves as held by God as well, we will never really know the joy of an intimate relationship with God and therefore of true faith and humility—of being a small cup held within a much larger one.

---

1. Sofia Cavalletti, *The Religious Potential of the Child 6–12 Years Old* (Chicago: Liturgy Training Publications, 2002): 8.

2. Ibid., 24.

3. *The Book of Common Prayer for the Episcopal Church* (New York: Oxford University Press, 1990): 363.

4. *The Roman Missal* (Washington, DC: International Commission on English in the Liturgy, Inc., 2010).

5. Robert Coles, *The Spiritual Life of Children* (Boston: Houghton Mifflin Co., 1990): xvi.

CHAPTER EIGHT

I Hope My Birthday Comes Soon

One way we invite the children to prayer at the end of each atrium session is by asking, "What would you like to say to Jesus?" Thanksgiving for everything from parents, toys, pets, and the color green is the prominent response, with older children also expressing prayers of petition: health for family, friends, and pets, strength to be kind to a mean classmate. Now and then, a child will simply blurt out a statement like, "I'm going to a party today!" or, "I lost a tooth!" or, "I got new shoes!" or, "I hope my birthday comes soon!"

Recently, I have been especially interested in the last statement, partly because it's been coming from some of the older children and partly because when one child says it, no one else repeats it. It has never turned into chaotic giggling about birthdays. All the other children seem to understand that anticipating one's birthday is sacred terrain. While adults tend to reprimand children for being so self-centered, their peers give only silent approval. I wonder what is going on in the children. I wonder what such a statement tells us about children's spirituality. I wonder what light such a candid and enthusiastic prayer might shine on our adult ways of praying.

Perhaps it means children are built for celebration. They get excited about the sticks and stones they find on the way home from school, about growing an inch or loosing a tooth or throwing a ball really high. Children measure life in terms of celebrations, big and little. Even as adults want them to learn to think of others, some egocentrism is appropriate. Children must experience the "specialness" that only birthdays convey in order to move out into the world in a loving way. They must know they are loved before they can love others. They must know joy before they can sacrifice. They must have their lives celebrated before they can celebrate someone else's life.

The gift children bring adults is the reminder that life is one continuing celebration. Everything we do and have and long for is for our enjoyment, not that we are to greedily consume everything in our midst, but that as children of God we recognize everything as a gift given to us. Then, we easily exclaim with child-like wonder: "I got new shoes!" or, "I'm going to a party!" or even, "I hope my birthday (or whatever else we really desire) comes soon!"

Thinking about this in the days approaching Advent and Christmas, I couldn't help but think of the children as prophets and angels, who announce the greatest of gifts—the birth of the Messiah, who is both child of Mary and Son of the Most High. The children's proclamation: "I hope my birthday comes soon!" clearly matches the excitement and anticipation of the prophet's proclamation: "Look, the young woman is with child and shall bear a son, and shall name him Immanuel" (Isaiah 7:14) and the multitude of angels singing, "Glory to God in the highest heaven" (Luke 2:14a). Neither prophet nor angel nor child can resist getting the word/Word out: We are deeply loved, loved like children; so "do not be afraid . . . for the Lord is with you . . . therefore rejoice" saying whatever you like to Jesus, including: "I hope my birthday comes soon!"

CHAPTER NINE

I Will Give My Soul and Life to the Lord

One day a seven-year-old boy came to me in the atrium and announced that he was going to write all the holy words in blue and all the regular words in black. I nodded as he continued on to a table. Soon he came back to me and said, "See?!" Then, showing me his paper, he read the large print spread across the center of it: "I AM GOD. I AM GESSUS." And just as he said, "GOD" and "GESSUS" were written in blue and the rest in black. The blue words were also surrounded by rays of yellow. After reading it to me, he seemed to catch himself and said, "Oh, but I'm not finished" and dashed off again. Returning a second time, he held his paper up and read the small print squeezed in across the very top: "I wil give my sol and lif to the Lord." His face was beaming as he trotted off again.

My immediate thought was, "That's what I've been trying to say and pray and do. How is it that this child could say aloud the very thing I can barely admit in the quiet of my own heart?" I was so deeply moved by this child's confident self-dedication that I've pondered it ever since—not so much about what he might have been saying about himself, but what it means for any of us to say, "I will give my soul and life to the Lord."

I have been particularly interested in the use of the phrase: "will give." I wonder why this child didn't say "I give . . . " but rather "I will give . . . ." How does the word *will* change the meaning? At its most basic level, the phrase "will give" points to a hope for the future or promise to God about the direction we plan to go with our life. At the same time, "will give" can be understood as a conditional phrase. This child could have been thinking: "I will give my soul and life to the Lord when I grow up, when I finish Sunday school, when I'm allowed to make my own decisions"—though I didn't detect any of these in him. Adults are more apt to use the conditional phrase, praying something like: "I will give my soul and life to you, O Lord, when I finish this project, when the children are grown, when my life is more organized and I'm not so busy, tired, frustrated." Or, "I will give my soul and life to you, O Lord, if you'll just let my child, friend, parent, spouse get better; if you'll just let me have this job, house, person, position; if you'll just let me catch my breath."

In all these scenarios, the emphasis is on something I plan, hope, or seek to do. When the child read his proclamation, however, there was nothing of this kind of straining forward. His life with God did not appear as an effort. Saying that he would give his soul and life to the Lord seemed to be the most natural thing in the world for him. If I had asked this seven-year-old about the difference between "I will give" and "I give," he most likely would not have been concerned about the difference. In fact, I can imagine him thinking there is no real difference. Only gradually have I been able to perceive this myself. Only gradually have I noticed that "I will give my soul and life to the Lord" is both a desire for the future and a daily fulfillment. In this moment I will give my whole self and for the whole rest of my life I will also give my soul and life to God.

Giving one's life to God, then, is not so much an act as it is a state of being. It is living in the awareness of the greater announcement of "I am God. I am Jesus." The ease with which they relate to God is perhaps one of the greatest gifts children bring to the rest of us. They are not worried about the future. They do not analyze their spiritual lives in the present. They just live it moment by moment.

Only recently have I realized that my attention has not really been on the difference between "give" and "will give," but on the "I," on what I will and will not give to God or to anyone. I read this proclamation as "I WILL give my soul and life to the Lord" whereas I think this child meant it as "I will GIVE my soul and life to the Lord." Or better yet: "I will G-I-V-E my soul and life to the Lord." Shifting the emphasis to giving reveals an expansiveness, a stretching in order to receive more of whatever it is that God has to give me, and an easy surrender to the One who knows me better than I know myself. It is as if this child is saying, "I will give myself over to this One I know in the deepest part of my being because I AM has spoken to me. I AM is so totally integrated into me that I do not need to strain, but only be still, only let I AM live in me."

I think this child's writing describes the essence of repentance, and can be helpful when we consider the season of Lent. Repentance involves easing into the given-ness and giving quality of God in Christ. While Lent is clearly a season for self-rededication, it begins with easing into the I AM—ness of God and easing into the "I AM" proclamations made by Jesus: "I am the Good Shepherd" who goes ahead of his sheep, seeking the lost and binding up the broken hearted. "I am the Light of the world," illuminating the darkness of oppression, illness, despair, cynicism, and doubt. "I am the Bread of Life" nourishing all with my unfailing presence. "I am the True Vine," uniting all people in their desire to write all the holy words in blue and sometimes scribbling on the edges of their consciousness, "I will give my soul and life to the Lord."

(This essay was published in *The Catechesis of the Good Shepherd Journal* 23 [2008]: 28–29.)

CHAPTER TEN

Naming the Atria

Throughout the history of Israel, being called by name has held enormous significance. Encounters with God often resulted in God changing people's names: Abram to Abraham, Sarai to Sarah, and Jacob to Israel. Jesus continues this rich tradition in the parable of the Good Shepherd. In doing so, he reminds us that being named and/or given a new name marks the beginning of a new moment in our life with God. It is a new invitation to listen and follow, to have the gift of God's unfailing presence lifted up for us so that we might respond with utter delight.

The beginning of the year in the Catechesis of the Good Shepherd brings us face to face with the theme of names and naming. In fact, the names given to the three atriums we have had in our church for some years now—the Good Shepherd Atrium, the True Vine Atrium, and the Saint Francis Atrium, correspond to the human questions that arise from knowing we are called by name. Sometimes spoken, often not, the three most basic questions all human beings ponder and that children ask in succession throughout the stages of childhood are: Who are you, Lord? Who are we? Who am I?

Very young children (those under age six) possess, what Sofia Cavalletti calls a mysterious knowledge of God. The child at this age knows there is "Another"—One who is above all and in all, who knows me by name and loves me more than anyone else does.

This child wants to know the name for the One who is already a reality in the child's life. It has been observed the world over that this child responds with serene joy upon hearing Jesus' proclamation, "I am the Good Shepherd." So our youngest atrium is called the Good Shepherd Atrium because the Good Shepherd is the answer to the youngest child's inner plea: "Who are you, Lord?"

Around age six, children become aware that life is complex and that human beings have a choice. They can either enrich the world by their words and actions or they can diminish it. Those who have experienced the love of Jesus the Good Shepherd want to respond with equal love. Their immediate question is: "Who are we?" That is, how do we make known the love we have known and enjoyed? How do we as members of the Good Shepherd's sheepfold live as collaborators with God? Jesus' proclamation: "I am the True Vine and you are the branches," answers these questions about the interrelatedness of all people, events and issues; and so we've named the atrium for the primary grade children the True Vine Atrium

Gradually, children ask the more personal question: "Who am I?" By age nine, children are making concrete choices about their present and future lives, actions, behaviors, and habits. This child is actively discerning his or her place in the world and role in the Kingdom of God. She or he is looking for role models, so the atrium for the older elementary grade child is called the Saint Francis Atrium because Francis of Assisi is one such model. While praying before the crucifix at San Damiano, he heard God tell him to "rebuild my church." At first Francis understood this to mean rebuild the churches that had become dilapidated. Later he understood God to be talking about people not buildings, and so it is with all of us. The children who know themselves to be called by name by Jesus the Good Shepherd are earnestly seeking out the particularities of their vocations in terms of contributing to the well-being of society. Their inner question is: Who am I? How am I called to contribute to the world? What are my particular gifts?

This fall, we are opening a fourth atrium, a second one to serve the unique religious capacities of the preschool and kindergarten children. One such capacity is that of wonder. Wonder is a force that pulls us forward, beckoning us to see deeper into reality, to pause as children do before the wonders of nature—ants making their way across the sidewalk, new shoots peeking out of the ground after a long winter's sleep, rain dripping from the gutter. All is wonderful and new to the littlest ones. Since the greatest reality of all is God, the Gospel, especially the parables of the Kingdom of God, captivates the youngest children's imagination. These parables initiate them into contemplation of the miracle of life, and if of life, then of God as well. Therefore, we are calling this new atrium the Mustard Seed Atrium because this is the first kingdom parable offered the youngest children. These little ones move easily between the concrete and transcendent realities, between seeing a tiny seed and seeing the power of life and wonder of God. These parables and the children who are so enamored by them remind us of the continual movement from less to more in the Kingdom of God—from death to life, from sadness to joy, from doubt to hope.

This evokes new yet very basic questions regarding our atria. As the physical environments of our atria grow and become more beautiful and more numerous, are we also being transformed? Is the change only external, or are there internal changes going on in us as well? As we eagerly incarnate the Word of God in tangible materials for the children, is it becoming more deeply etched in our own hearts and lives? Or are we so busy congratulating ourselves for our fine work, beautiful atria, and excellent programs that we've ceased to hear the Good Shepherd calling us to be true servants to children—persons who desperately want to know in that deepest sense of knowing: Who are you, Lord? Who are we? Who am I?

CHAPTER ELEVEN

Like a Kiss from God

We were sitting in a circle on the floor, the children and I. Before us on a low table covered with a white linen cloth, lay the familiar signs of Baptism—a paschal candle, several smaller candles, a bowl of water, a small white gown, a Bible, and a small container of oil called Holy Chrism. We had all seen and touched these items many times before, wondering at the Light of Christ that is given to all, feeling the refreshing water poured over our hands, reveling in the words of the Good Shepherd: "I call my sheep by name," and enjoying the fragrance of Holy Chrism. Everything was the same, yet it was all new as well.

Eight-year-old Angela had been baptized during the summer, and this was our first chance to gaze upon these signs of divine life and love since that moment. It was one of those peaceful yet chatty sessions. The children had much to say, showed great delight in these things that reveal God's unfailing presence, and were clearly happy for Angela. As for Angela, she handled each item with great care. It seemed she was remembering and savoring the past as well as the present. After a while she said, "I like the oil best of all." Then with some hesitation, she continued, "This might sound silly." But her confidence outweighed any embarrassment as she announced, "It's like getting a kiss from God." No one thought it was silly. No one said a thing. Nodding heads confirmed the truth of Angela's declaration. I, too, was rendered silent, for this child had summed up every theology of Baptism that had ever been conceived.

I have taken courses on the history of Baptism in graduate school, its development throughout the centuries and the various theological perspectives held along the way, but not one captivated me like this child's one sentence proclamation of the essence of this great sacrament. Can it be that Baptism is essentially God's desire to show us we are loved completely? Yes, I think it is just that. It is a kiss from God, a tender gesture of love, an assurance of forgiveness of sin, and a hope that the essence of the moment will sustain us throughout all our days.

Angela, like everyone, will discover soon enough that responding with equal tenderness toward those around her is not as simple as giving a kiss. Our baptism vows are demanding. Resisting evil, proclaiming the Gospel, serving Christ in others, and striving for justice and peace are arduous and complicated affairs. And yet, because it was experienced as a kiss, as an explicit gesture of a loving relationship, perhaps Angela's baptismal journey will be different. Perhaps living out her baptismal vows will be simpler and easier, or at least more integrated into the whole of her life, because she has experienced what Maria Montessori calls the first moment of learning—the moment of captivation. It is a moment that often goes unnamed in traditional education, but which is essential for the full assimilation of all knowledge.

According to Montessori, learning consists of two moments. The first moment is the full person experience, the "ah ha!" It is a moment of complete captivation, when we are completely taken by an object and all our faculties are engaged—mind, heart, emotions, soul, and body. We feel a kind of leap forward, a quietness, an opening up, and a slowing down. Everything else dissolves; and we are held by the beauty of one thing. Sunsets and symphonies, stars and seashells, views from mountaintops and sights seen only under a microscope—are things that hold me spell-bound. It is an affective experience, one that involves a person's whole being, and one in which the person may not even be aware that she or he is being drawn forward in awe. It is sometimes called the moment of setting afire the heart of the person or of falling in love with the beauty and wonder of life in front of us.

This moment, however, must be followed by a second moment, by an objective exploration of the object before us. This is the moment of discriminating thought. In this moment, there is a distance between the person and the object. For instance, engaging in a study of the atmospheric elements and conditions that cause the vast array of colors at the end of the day might follow the experience of seeing a sunset. We need not move children from one moment to the other hastily, yet both moments are necessary for lasting learning to occur. The first without the second leaves knowledge on the superficial plane where it easily dissipates; and the second without the first makes learning rootless and dry and easily forgotten. The absence of either moment robs a person of the personal motivation, inner satisfaction, and enduring memory that true learning yields.

For Angela, her "kiss from God" needs the later experience of studying and discerning the specifics of the baptismal covenant in relation to her life as well as conscious reflection on the many occasions in which water, oil, and light have been used throughout time in Scripture and liturgy. For instance, linking the anointing with oil in Baptism with the anointing of Israel's kings roots the initial baptismal experience in the larger context of salvation history. The divine hope for Israel as enacted in the anointing of its kings becomes one's own hope, for it helps one understand and live into the responsibility attached to the vocation of being an heir to the kingdom of God.

In the first moment, a relationship is established. In the second moment, that relationship is expanded, even tested. The connections made and knowledge gleaned help solidify the first moment. In the process, it changes from being a mere pleasurable experience to one that motivates one's life. In her prolonged observation of children, Sofia Cavalletti concludes that the experience of falling in love with the Good Shepherd is the true source of the moral life. The realization of being loved by God becomes the yardstick by which one's actions are measured and evokes true remorse when one fails to respond adequately to the gift of God's love in real life situations.

Together, the first and second moments of learning form and inform a person, integrating experience and knowledge deep within a person. That new knowledge becomes itself another first moment, another "ah ha" and the cycle repeats itself. The embrace of love Angela experienced becomes the springboard for a whole continuing cycle of first and second moments—a whole series of additional experiences of contemplation and study of the gift of God in the sacrament of Baptism and elsewhere.

In the early Church, catechumens followed a similar process of experience of the sacraments followed by broader instruction and exploration of their meaning. This catechetical process is called mystagogy. Some instruction was given before Baptism, but Baptism itself was believed to be the primary mode of understanding and initiation. Most instruction was reserved for after the event of Baptism. At that time the newly baptized were helped to reflect on their baptismal experience—on their "kiss from God." In this way, experience took precedence over teaching. In his treatise, "On the Instruction of Beginners," Augustine of Hippo points out the essence of instructing people in the Christian life and faith, saying "the main purpose of instruction is to give the catechumen the inner experience of the revelation of God's love as anticipated in the Old Testament and manifested in Jesus Christ."[1] In other words, initiation into the truths of the Christian faith involved initiation through the sacraments rather than initiation to the sacraments. It wasn't until the formulation of Christian doctrines in the fourth and fifth centuries that pre-baptismal instruction in Christian doctrine became prevalent.

The Second Vatican Council's reinstitution of the catechu-menate is an attempt to return to the mystagogical method of the early Church. Its aim is to help people have an experience of the mystery of divine presence. In fact, the whole of the Judeo-Christian tradition is founded on documenting experiences of God. From the crossing of the Red Sea to Christ's Death and Resurrection, faith is a matter of anticipating, experiencing, recognizing, nam-ing, remembering, sharing, and celebrating the presence of God in human history. Angela's confident description of her baptismal experience reveals the essence of mystagogy: initiating people into the mysteries of Christ. The "kiss" is just the beginning, but a very significant beginning. Much more is yet to come, not only for Angela, but for all who continue pondering the mystery of God in Christ with her.

I. Robert Ulrich, *A History of Religious Education: Documents and Interpretations from the Judaeo-Christian Tradition* (New York: New York University Press, 1968): 47.

CHAPTER TWELVE

Your Enemies Are Like the Stars

Eight-year-old Lauren rarely comes to the atrium. When she does come, she always works quietly alongside her friend Rachel from school. I often wonder what she can be absorbing when she comes so infrequently. Today Lauren and Rachel set about copying the maxims, short sayings like: "[Forgive] not seven times, but, I tell you, seventy times seven" (Matthew 18:21) and "Be perfect as your heavenly Father is perfect" (Matthew 5:48). They worked quietly, so I didn't pay much attention to them. At the end of the atrium time Lauren handed me a piece of paper with these words printed on it: "Your enemies are like the stars in the sky. You should love them." As always, I was shocked into silence, but also too curious to remain so for long. Trying to hold back my curiosity and excitement, I asked her why she decided to write the maxim: "Love your enemies" this way. She shrugged her shoulders and said she didn't know. I told her it was beautiful and made a mental note to talk to her mom. When I asked her mom whether Lauren might have heard this phrase at home or in school, she said no. The next week I asked Lauren the same questions I asked her mom. Had they been talking in school about loving others or being friends or discussing what an enemy is? Again, she gave a negative response. "I just thought it up on my own," she said.

She thought it up on her own. Some thing or some One within her prompted her to take the all too familiar maxim, "love your enemies," and turn it into poetry, a riddle, an invitation. Since the day I read those words on Lauren's paper, I've wondered what they might mean. How are enemies like the stars in the sky? Stars are far away, beautiful, mysterious, flecks of light. Can our enemies be these same things? Is this child suggesting that we examine the dark corners of our lives and prejudices, noticing our perceived enemies for what they really are—possible sources of light, beauty, and understanding, and worthy of our love? In her reformulated maxim I hear echoes of Isaiah's prophetic announcement:

> For my thoughts are not your thoughts,
>   nor my ways your ways, says the LORD.
> For as the heavens are higher than the earth,
>   so are my ways higher than your ways,
>   and my thoughts than your thoughts.
>
> For as rain and snow come down from heaven,
>   and do not return there until they have watered the earth,
> making it bring forth and sprout,
>   giving seed for the sower and bread to the eater
> so shall my word be that goes out from my mouth;
>   it shall not return to me empty,
> but it shall accomplish that which I purpose,
>   and succeed in the thing for which I sent it.
> (Isaiah 55:8–11)

What prophetic announcement is Lauren making that I cannot discern? Can it be that our enemies—those who oppress, who abuse power, who scam the innocent, who kill and steal and cheat people are flecks of light rather than causes of the darkness in our world? "My ways are not your ways says the LORD." Can it be that this seven-year-old child, like God, sees the light hidden within the darkness of our enemies?

. . . even the darkness is not dark to you;
 the night is as bright as the day
 for darkness is as light to you.
(Psalm 139:12)

Does she possess the divine hope that light, however minuscule, remains alive in the hardest of hearts?

Do not remember the former things,
or consider the things of old.
I am about to do a new thing;
 now it springs forth, do you not perceive it?
 I will make a way in the wilderness
and rivers in the desert.
(Isaiah 43:18–21)

How often do we not perceive the new things God is doing because the announcement comes from the mouths of babes?

For instance, it occurs to me that the command to "love your enemies" tells us what to do, what action is necessary, but "Your enemies are like the stars in the sky; you should love them" describes the enemy before suggesting action. It coaxes a relationship, reminding us that, though distant, our enemies are also sheep of the Good Shepherd and branches on the True Vine. More importantly, Lauren's maxim puts the enemy first, echoing the divine order in the Kingdom of God: "the first shall be last and the last first" (Matthew 19:30, Mark 10:31, Luke 13:30). Also by making an analogy, Lauren shifts the original maxim from an abstract dictum to a visible parable, reminding all that the commandments serve as invitations to live within the kingdom of God with greater authenticity, joy, and attention to one's neighbor.

It is as if Lauren took the teaching model so familiar in the synoptic Gospels with their numerous maxims and moral parables and expanded it until it became a sign of the mystical union dominating John's account of the Gospel. This should not surprise me since Sofia Cavalletti found that the relational quality of the parable of the Good Shepherd resonates deeply within children all around the globe. Perhaps Lauren needed the added dimension of relationship in the maxims and not finding it, created it herself.

Whatever her reasons and whatever her maxim means to her or those who ponder it, this child's rewriting of this maxim highlights Sofia Cavalletti's insistence on adults assuming the role of the unprofitable servant. That is, catechists cannot take credit for what emerges in the children's artwork or verbal responses because the Word we proclaim is not our own. Therefore, any fruit that comes forth is also not our own. And that fruit is so often much greater than anything we could have ever imagined.

At the turn of the twentieth century, Maria Montessori lamented the self-congratulatory tendency in many teachers, saying that adult self-centeredness reveals a lack of a sense of wonder and appreciation for the inherent capabilities of children. Typically, when children exhibit some significant cognitive advance, adults attribute it to their own efforts and own clever pedagogy when, in fact, it is the child who is to be admired. If we can put aside our adult-centered perspectives and anxieties and see the child's spontaneous development as one of the unique mysteries of life, which occurs through the power of the Holy Spirit, then we can be drawn forward in wonder and assume the role of servant with ease and gladness of heart. When we understand that children's innate ability to learn and grow of their own accord is a function of the Holy Spirit, then we can perceive the necessary shift in the role of the adult from that of giving direct instruction to that of preparing the environment so that the child can develop according to the divinely-ordained stages of growth and development. With our gaze on the child rather than on ourselves or our programs, the questions we ask change. Instead of asking: what do children need to learn or how can we measure the effectiveness of particular methods of instruction, our questions become ones that reveal a sense of wonder and respect. Who is the child? What characteristics is she or he revealing? What are his or her religious capabilities? What is she or he asking me to provide? Instead of focusing on creative teaching methods, education should be about investigating "the wonderful powers of divine creation in the child's soul."[1]

---

1. Maria Montessori, *The Child in the Church*, ed. E.M. Standing (Saint Paul: North Central Publishing Co., 1965): 5.

CHAPTER THIRTEEN

The Presents of God

"Here's the presents of God!" exclaimed a six-year-old boy as he held up his paint-soaked paper that he covered with an assortment of squares and rectangles in blue and green with red and yellow squiggles running through them. As he spoke, paint dripped off the bottom of his paper and onto the linoleum floor at our feet. I must have looked as bewildered as I felt because he went on to say, "You know, the presents of God, just like you said." I had just spoken to the group about the "presence" of God, but this child heard "presents."

Since that moment, I've often wondered about children's mistakes like this. Clearly this child misunderstood the idea of the presence of God I was trying to present, or did he? Can it be that by confusing *presence* with *presents* he actually clarified the abstract theological concept of the presence of God? Can it be that he understands more than he knows or I imagine? Can it be that, by living in the stage of concrete operations as described by Piaget, children recognize God's presence as presents, as very tangible gifts? Can it be that adults like me can say children are gifts to us, but never really recognize them as a gift of divine presence or more specifically, as the mouth-piece of God?

It makes me realize that Dawn Devries, professor of systematic theology at Presbyterian School of Christian Education, is right. There is a shadow side to developmental theories. While recognizing the uniqueness of childhood, Piaget's stages of cognitive development and Lawrence Kohlberg's stages of moral development "tend to distance adults from children, so that the child is seen as an 'other' rather than as a fellow human being."[1] This "otherness" is revealed in the consistent inference that childhood is a period of deficiency and "earlier phases of development are taken as relatively less valuable than later phases. . . . The infant is valuable chiefly for the toddler he will become, the young child for the adolescent, the teenager for the adult."[2]

In contrast to traditional developmental theories, Maria Montessori recognized the fact that children are not just on their way to adulthood, but are real gifts to adults. She invites us to look at adults and children "as two different forms of human life going on at the same time and exerting upon one another a reciprocal influence."[3] In *The Child in the Church*, Montessori expounds on this theme. What she says is so strikingly true that I refer to this quotation often:

> Let us imagine for a while that the world consisted only of
> adults, because man was born already developed and mature;
> and because of this could dispense with parents. The most basic
> community, the family, which of all natural communities exerts
> a deeper and more lasting influence on the spirit of man, and
> which sets itself up both by means of, and because of the child
> with his many needs, would then have no more reason to exist.
> Not only would this profoundly change our manner of life, but it
> would also change man himself. The tender, intimate, affectionate,
> reverent, adaptable and familiar sentiments of the heart, which
> unfold through the many years of relationship between child
> and parent, would be replaced by entirely different characteristics.
> Not only would the children of men be different but also the
> parent themselves.
>
> It is just through his condition of being a son that the child
> is able to change, for the good, the adults around him. Is not the
> life of self-forgetfulness and sacrificing love which centers around
> the child and the satisfaction of his needs something which is at

once noble, uplifting and character-building? The child is indeed not conscious of his formative influence on the adults, and therefore does not consider himself as an apostle. But what is proper to the child—his natural innocence, his affection, his self-abandon, his defenseless condition and his touching appeal for help, his timorous cry when he finds himself alone or in danger—all of these marvelously move the human heart.

The child can change the hearts of men; in the midst of children their hardness disappears. The child can annihilate selfishness and awaken the spirit of sacrifice . . . In this way does God move and form the adult through the child.[4]

Here, Montessori names the key to perceiving children as gifts. It's as simple as realizing that adults need children as much as children need adults. This is mutual blessing; and where both the presence and presents of God are found.

---

1. Dawn Devries, "Toward a Theology of Childhood," *Interpretation* 55, no. 2 (2001): 163.

2. Ibid.

3. Maria Montessori, *The Child in the Church*, ed. E.M. Standing (Saint Paul: North Central Publishing Co., 1965): 7.

4. Ibid., 8–9.

CHAPTER FOURTEEN

The Gifts of God for the People of God

Why is it that the most familiar, stable things get turned upside down when put in the hands of children? Such was the case recently when a small group of children scrambling around on the atrium floor assembled a rather involved timeline depicting salvation history as a continuous progression of gifts. Beginning with samples of the gifts of God hidden in the depths of the earth, observable in nature, evident in other people, and finally visible in Jesus who is present to us in the Eucharist, it becomes evident that everything around us is gathered up and present on the altar each time we come to the Eucharist.

When this time line is completed, we give children in the Episcopal Church a narrow text strip with the prayer of invitation to communion: "The gifts of God for the people of God" and invite them to place it wherever they like on the time line. In other words, what is the best way to show that all that we have and all that we are comes with us to the Eucharist? Immediately a child took the strip, walked back to the start of the time line, placed it there triumphantly and announced: "It's a welcome sign. You know, like at a zoo or museum." All the other children agreed, insisting that everyone else in the atrium come and see. And sure enough, looking at the time line from the end rather than the side as I had imagined it should go, these familiar words appeared as a clear and expansive welcome.

The timeline and the children's work with it exemplify the Montessori way of teaching called cosmic education. This method resembles an hourglass. We offer a large view of salvation history with timelines first and then examine individual events and people such as creation, the Exodus, the prophets, Jesus, and ourselves as they fit into the whole expanse of history, and wonder at the fact that everyone and everything is connected. The essence of cosmic education lies in the awareness that everything in the universe is linked in some way. Like pearls on a golden thread, all people and events hang together—individual yet united by the eternal love of God in Christ. It is as if innumerable invisible bridges connect all people. The work, inventions, and discoveries of previous generations benefit us today. And who knows how our medical discoveries and constantly developing technologies, our art and our music, will effect future generations?

Presenting timelines of the history of the kingdom of God to children six to nine years old as a unity and as a progression of gifts matches this age child's desire for an expansive view of life and society. These primary age children are no longer satisfied with separate stories of the life of Christ or his teachings, or examining the individual sacramental signs. Now, they want us to help them pull everything together under larger umbrellas and themes. Therefore, beginning when children are six, we offer synthesis work. This is work that compares and contrasts sets of parables, stories of Jesus' birth, or prophecies, or places all prayers from the Eucharist in order as they occur in the Mass. In addition, we observe specific themes such as light, the Holy Spirit, prayer, and growth in the stories of Jesus' birth and the parables.

Likewise, the elementary grade children, those nine to twelve years old, know that life is complex and are eager to penetrate this complexity so that they can begin considering their place in the society. The timeline offered to these children is called the Plan of

God. It depicts the rise and fall, contributions and failures, of civilizations from ancient times to the present and on to the Parousia, or second coming of Christ. With the Plan of God timeline, we can easily see how civilizations come and go but the work of their hearts, minds, and hands gets passed on to future generations as gifts or inheritances. Basically, it gives a theological perspective to the social studies classes in which these children are currently involved in school, evoking awe, wonder, gratitude, and a desire to enhance society with one's own life.

All these timelines depicting salvation history do indeed act as welcome signs, inviting children and adults alike into further and deeper consideration of the mystery and gift of living our particular moment in time with a renewed sense of purpose and much delight. Can we imagine the empty tomb as a welcome sign as well? Jesus' Resurrection is surely an invitation into a new vision, understanding, and openness to God's plan for giving "the gifts of God for the people of God."

CHAPTER FIFTEEN

Can We Read More?

After reading about and pondering Jesus' arrest in the Garden of Olives with a group of primary grade children, I asked if anyone had any other thoughts or questions. With quiet hope, one six-year-old boy asked, "Can we read more?" Time was short, but we continued reading. How could I say no when this child as well as his classmates looked at me with great earnestness? What was it that stirred in them? Of all the things I thought they might say, this was not one of them. Why was I so surprised by their desire to read more Scripture? Some of their parents have asked me how they should talk to their children about Jesus dying, and here were the children asking to hear more, pleading to be let in on the truth. I was reminded of Gretchen Wolff Pritchard's words:

> The cross is a mystery and a terror; we feel we would gladly
> shield our children from it. But I have found that children
> do not want to be shielded from the cross. Stumbling block and
> folly though it may be to grown-ups, to children, the cross is the
> power and wisdom of God.
>
> Children know that the world is full of terror, that no
> answers are easy, that no comfort comes without cost, pain, and
> mystery. It is not the cross that terrifies children, but the false
> Gospel that bypasses the cross and leaves us forever alone with
> our pain and guilt, and the false Gospel of optimism that tries
> to assure us that Adam and Eve are still in the garden among the
> tame animals, and there is nothing outside.[1]

These are startling words, yet Sofia Cavalletti confronts adults even more directly:

> There is the conviction, often unexpressed verbally, that the child is not capable of receiving such great realities. I believe the truth to be otherwise. It is we who have not managed to transmit these realities to children with the essentiality which is necessary, and the assumed incapacity of the child becomes an excuse to cover our ignorance and to exempt us from further and deeper research.[2]

Now I am beginning to understand Cavalletti's insistence on continued study of Holy Scripture. During a visit with her in Rome in May of 2005, she told me at least five times, "The Word is the most important thing." I had been trying to coax her into conversation about the transformation that often occurs in adults as a result of becoming involved in the Catechesis of the Good Shepherd. She responded rather off-handedly, "Yes, but the Word is the most important thing." Not to be deterred, I inquired about Jesus saying adults must become as children if they are to enter into the kingdom of heaven (Matthew 18:3). Wouldn't it be important to articulate adults' journey in this work as well? More emphatically she said, "No, that's not what this is about. The Word is the most important thing." When I went on to say how grateful I am for having been introduced to this work and how much it's meant to me, she continued, "That's very nice, but you know, dear, the Word is the most important thing."

Just as the general population assumes children cannot comprehend the paschal mystery, the idea of adults continuing their own formation in the Christian life and faith through further and deeper study in Scripture, liturgy, and child development comes as an equal surprise. Yet even the briefest observation of church personnel reveals another startling fact: the people with the most theological education are the most removed from children.

When I asked Sofia what she hoped would continue when she was no longer around, she said, "That people would still observe the child." She said nothing about the Catechesis of the Good

Shepherd continuing or growing or being kept pristine. Her only concern was continued attention to the Word and the child. How hard it is to forget one's self and attend to what is most important! How often am I more concerned with getting the catechetical materials made than with pondering the Word I am to proclaim with them? How often I worry about children missing presentations and subsequently fail to observe those who are present. As a result, I am always surprised when the children fidget during introductions to a piece of Scripture but quickly quiet down once the Word is read from the Bible. If I really believed God's Word, and not my performance, was the most important thing, I would not be surprised by children like Joel who chose copying Scripture with his dad during an Atrium Open House over the craft projects I put out.

Again and again, children point toward the centrality of the Word of God. At one point, even the three dimensional clay figures and corresponding dioramas depicting the events surrounding Jesus' birth sat on the atrium shelf completely untouched all year. Instead, the children only wanted to read from the Bible. Their plea: "Can we read more?" echoed through every atrium session. It seems they are fervently asking me to see them as they really are— tremendously capable of and in need of pondering the paschal mystery. They are asking parents and teachers to continue their own religious formation by attending adult education classes in their parishes, Catechesis of the Good Shepherd courses, diocesan workshops, and graduate level courses in Scripture and liturgy.

It is interesting that I began my master's degree in theology so that I might be better equipped to answer questions posed by adults in the Catechesis of the Good Shepherd formation courses. Now I see the children's request to read more of the Passion narratives as a more necessary, even if less glamorous, need. Now many years later, I hear a barely perceptible invitation beneath the children's hesitant question, "Can we read more?" In addition to wanting to know more of the story of Jesus' Death and Resurrection themselves, they want to know if I will read more so that I can better facilitate our meditations. Will I continue my own study and prayer of the life of Christ? Will I prepare myself with the most important thing—the Word of God—so that I can assist adults and children in a common religious experience based on children's religious capacities?

I. Gretchen Wolff Pritchard, *Offering the Gospel to Children* (Cambridge, MA: Cowley Publications, 1992): 4.

2. Sofia Cavalletti, *The Religious Potential of the Child* (Chicago: Liturgy Training Publications, 1992): 51.

CHAPTER SIXTEEN

We Look Like God

Whenever I reflect with elementary age children on the Genesis 1:26 passage: "Let us make humankind in our image, according to our likeness . . . ," they always say, "We look like God" or as one child put it: "Now I know what God looks like." I've wondered if by saying we look like God the children mean we share a similar physical appearance or that we exhibit similar behaviors as in possessing creativity or compassion like God. When I press them on this, they always say it refers to physical features. To children, our very faces are the face of God. Any similarity in behavior appears to be secondary in their minds.

Is this a sign of infantile understanding of Scripture and humankind and typical childhood egocentricity? Do we dismiss their interpretation as childish and immature, perhaps correcting them so they will learn to be good? Or is it just possible that children speak a truth adults seldom recognize, which is the great dignity given to us human creatures? We often talk about being Christ in the world, but that is always connected to our actions, not our facial features.

When the children talk about being made in the image of God as meaning we bear the face of God, they are neither silly nor arrogant. Instead they seem to possess a hidden knowledge, one that originates in some inner wisdom. Children seem to move easily between the visible and invisible and so I wonder if, to them, there really is no difference between God's face and ours. Therefore, the Genesis text about humankind being made in the image of God is totally and easily linked in children's minds to the Incarnation, that mystery whereby the face of a child is in fact the very face of God.

The children's confident assertion that we look like God and God looks like us seems the perfect point of departure for our approaching journey through Advent. As we resume our singing of "O Come, O Come Emmanuel," are we not becoming as children again? Full of confident hope, we eagerly look forward to knowing once again the mystery of Emmanuel—God with a face like ours.

CHAPTER SEVENTEEN

A Child's Icon of Unity

We all know that a picture paints a thousand words, and this drawing that a ten-year-old child made many years ago reveals the truth of this dictum. She brought it to me saying: "God is looking at Jesus looking at us." Notice the interweaving of the face of God and the cross which forms the nose. The smile, also, radiates out from the base. God and Jesus appear as one and we, the viewers, are being drawn into this scene as well so that we might become one with it, too.

It is as if this child were trying to depict Jesus' prayer in the Gospel according to John: "The glory that you have given me I have given them so that they may be one as we are one" (John 17:21–22). It is as if this child wrote an icon for us, so that we can perceive what she and Jesus perceive—oneness, communion, and complete unity.

If we can get past our own giddy nervousness when faced with the blunt honesty and crude simplicity of children's drawings, a lot of their artwork acts as icons. With their distorted perspectives and exaggerated features, children's drawings mirror the same techniques used in Eastern Orthodox icons.

Icons are said to be "written" rather than "painted," following strict rules about colors, type of paint, and proportions. While their perspective is often skewed, making them appear flat, the eyes are always penetrating. Most of all, icons are meant to be prayed with, to be pondered, to be still in front of, so the truth they contain can enter and convert our hearts, particularly the truth of the deep current of life and love emanating from God and running throughout all of history.

Nearly a hundred years ago, Maria Montessori spoke about this underlying current of divine life in the universe. She called it an "Intelligence of Love" that is moving all people and all creation toward complete unity, or as she called it, "cosmic communion." She was particularly disturbed that all sorts of technology was being put into weapons and war but there was no science for peace. She believed only a new education of children, which she called cosmic education, could bring about peace. She says:

> this concept [cosmic communion] must not be presented as some
> ideal imposed upon humankind in order to judge their actions,
> but as a pre-existent reality which is constantly unfolding. We are
> not talking about the forcing of human beings to cooperate with
> each other so as to be united. [Rather,] we are speaking about

elevating human consciousness to something that already exists and demands that human beings consciously adapt to the real state of things in which they live.[1]

Just as the Jesus of John's account of the Gospel insists that he does not do his own will but the will of him who sent him, so, too, human beings cannot create peace or unity, or end hunger, disease, or war alone. In fact, most of our attempts have fallen quite short. Instead, humanity must step way back—so far back that we can transcend the immediate and fragmented present. Only from an objective view point can we detect the deep current running through reality and history.

If we can do this, we will perceive a marvelous web of interactions at work in the universe—a network of exchanges among people all around the world and between human beings and the earth—that makes life possible, rich, rewarding, and expansive. This network of exchanges of thoughts, services, and goods includes not only people alive today, but all those who have come before us as well as those yet to be born. Just think for a moment of the person or people thousands of years ago who first cultivated plants like wheat or first domesticated animals or first created the wheel and all the ways in which we have received their work as an inheritance, a gift. It is these exchanges of knowledge and goods that Montessori calls cosmic communion. It is as if there are thousands, even millions, of invisible bridges linking people with people throughout the ages.

Picking up on Montessori's thesis, Sofia Cavalletti opens her book *History's Golden Thread* with this summary statement: "There has always been a plan in the mind of God the aim of which is to bring all of humanity and all of creation to full enjoyment of the life of God."[2]

Can we perceive in this child's icon the joy inherent in living in cooperation with God's plan for cosmic communion? Do we dare let these eyes open our own eyes so that we can perceive God calling forth peace and unity in the world—one that is not of our own making, but still requires our participation? How do we tell the difference between the current of divine life at work in the world and our dreams and efforts to bring about justice, peace, and unity? How do we relax into this flow of life? One clue lies in the gift or ability to be in awe and wonder at the universe. In the atria we strive to nurture the natural wonder children already possess. Sofia Cavalletti speaks of wonder this way:

> The nature of wonder is not a force that pushes us passively from behind; it is situated ahead of us and attracts us with irresistible force toward the object of our astonishment; it makes us advance toward it, filled with enchantment.
>
> Wonder is a dynamic value; nevertheless it does not drive us to activism but draws us to activity, to an activity we do as persons immersed in the contemplation of something that exceeds us. Maybe the particularity of wonder is that we find activity and contemplation inseparably blended within it.[3]

This unity between contemplation and activity comes easily to children. They see something and they want to touch, taste, smell, and know more about it. So, in the atria we offer an education to wonder, an education to the vastness of history and God's presence within it, an education to the history of the kingdom of God as a history of gifts. Only after striking the imagination from these enormous vistas do we go to the particulars. Only with a deep sense of wonder of the universe and the underlying Intelligence of Love directing it can any of us choose our work and our place within it.

Linked with the capacity of wonder is being open to the gift and power of the Holy Spirit. For Pentecost, the feast of the Holy Spirit, in the atrium we have, as in church, a beautiful celebration of the gifts of the Holy Spirit as articulated in Isaiah 11: 2–3a:

> The spirit of the LORD shall rest on him,
>> the spirit of wisdom and understanding,
>> the spirit of counsel and might,
>> the spirit of knowledge and the fear of the LORD.
> His delight shall be in the fear of the LORD.

One year, a child came to me the week before Pentecost and asked me to name these seven gifts. After I went through them with him, he said, "Last year I asked for wisdom and received it, so this year I'm going to ask for knowledge." Can we be as bold, as confident, or as excited as him? Can we be as articulate as another child who wrote:

> . . . I would like to know for sure that before God and my neighbor I am a good, noble, respectable woman with a light that cannot be put out, like the light God gave me when I was born that gets stronger in Communion. I know that someday when God calls me and I give my effort to it, I will succeed at being a messenger of peace.[4]

May we all ask for and receive the gifts we need to perceive and live in conjunction with God's plan for cosmic communion. May we be filled with wisdom and wonder. May we be one with the Father, Son, and Holy Spirit.

I. Maria Montessori, *Cosmic Education,* quoted in *The Religious Potential of the Child, 6–12 Years Old* (Chicago: Liturgy Training Publications, 2002): 33.

2. Sofia Cavalletti, *History's Golden Thread: The History of Salvation,* trans. Rebekah Rojcewicz (Chicago: Liturgy Training Publications, 1999): 4.

3. Sofia Cavalletti, *The Religious Potential of the Child* (Chicago: Liturgy Training Publications, 1992): 138-139.

4. Sofia Cavalletti, *The Religious Potential of the Child 6 to 12 Years Old* (Chicago: Liturgy Training Publications, 2002): 40.

CHAPTER EIGHTEEN

My Favorite Part

When an eight-year-old child brought a Bible to me and asked me to help him find the story of the three kings or magi, I did so without pause. As we turned to the second chapter in the Gospel of Matthew where the account is located, he casually said, "I like this story. My favorite part is when they worship him." Then he took the Bible and went off to read it alone. I could not have been more surprised.

Never in my entire life have I heard anyone expound on the magi worshipping Jesus. Never in my wildest dreams have I imagined a child would say that is his or her favorite part of the story. I have never focused on that moment with children in the atrium. And yet, surely the magi's act of worshipping the Christ child is the critical moment, the climax of the story, and the whole point of their journey of following a particular star and bringing gifts. They had a plan, a simple one: go and pay homage to the newborn King of the Jews. How they got there, who they met on the way, why they brought the gifts they did remain secondary. And this child knows this. A mere eight-year-boy adores the adoring of the three magi. He loves watching them quietly bow down and worship the King of Kings. I imagine he knows that their relationship, their desire to offer homage to Jesus, is akin to his own desire and experience. Can we know the same? What keeps us from lifting up this moment with children? Why do we stay on the superficial plane, having children make crowns and stars? Why do we herd children so readily toward making a moral response, asking them to consider what gifts Jesus wants from them? How will this change my next meditation with children on this account? How do I make space for children to enter this central moment of the story with the same clear devotion as this child? After twenty plus years in various atria can I finally be a non-anxious presence there just like this child?

Is Jesus referring to the child's non-anxious relationship with God and unselfconscious declarations about this relationship when he says, "Unless you change and become like children, you will never enter the Kingdom of heaven" (Matthew 18:3)? Perhaps Jesus is saying, "Unless you relax into your role as one of my sheep you will continue wasting your time comparing yourselves to one another, arguing among yourselves, demeaning each other, and struggling to be independently happy. Unless you are 'still and know that I am God' (Psalm 46:10), you will always be anxious. Unless your main aim in life is honoring God, you will never make adoration your favorite part."

CHAPTER NINETEEN

The Empty Tomb

Two new seven-year-old children came to the atrium this week. After showing them around, they went straight to the wooden and plaster model of the empty tomb tucked away on the bottom shelf at the far end of the atrium. Taking it out they gently examined each figure: the man dressed in white and the three women who had come to anoint Jesus' body. As I told them the story of Jesus' Resurrection, they kept asking who the man in white is. So I read the accompanying Scripture booklet and began my usual line of wondering questions: I wonder what it was like for these women whose dear friend had died? I wonder what they thought when they found the tomb empty? I wonder what made it possible for Jesus to rise from the dead? I wonder if this reminds you of any of the parables Jesus' taught? But these children were not interested in my line of thinking. They continued pondering the identity of the man dressed in white; and they offered their own ideas: "Maybe he's the one who put Jesus to death and he came to say he's sorry." "Maybe he's the one who made Jesus alive again." "Maybe he's Jesus' friend."

I invited them to listen again to the announcement the man makes, "Do not be alarmed; you are looking for Jesus of Nazareth, who was crucified. He has been raised. Look, there is the place they laid him" (Mark 16:5–6). Striving to help the children identify the man in white, I asked, "When else have we heard someone say, 'Do not be afraid?'" and "When else have we seen a messenger from God come and make a grand announcement?" I was thinking of the angel who came to Mary to tell her she would be the mother of Jesus. Again the children indicated they had something else on their minds. They were not in a hurry to find an answer. They seemed to enjoy, in a very serious way, asking, "Who could the man in white be?"

Once again I witnessed children viewing a Scripture passage from a different perspective. It seemed these children were not as interested in the miracle of the Resurrection as with the relationship between the man in white and Jesus. Do children instinctively know that death and resurrection is the normal cycle of life and therefore do not need to contemplate it further? Do they have a clearer idea of the essentiality of relationship in regard to the resurrection? Their questions always pushed toward an understanding of the relationship between the man in white and Jesus; and that relationship centered on forgiveness.

Why is it that these children who had never been in an atrium before went straight for the materials that proclaim the central truth of the Christian faith? The model of the empty tomb was nearly hidden from view. I did not point it out to them when I showed them around because I thought they needed to become acquainted with other, less intense works first. Why is it that I cannot imagine children new to the atrium as being able to receive the essence of our faith? Perhaps it is because it is also hard to imagine that the Kingdom of God is like a tiny seed or a little bit of leaven, a precious pearl or a mere child. Perhaps it is because I nod knowingly, but without really understanding, at Jesus' prayer: "I thank you, Father, Lord of heaven and earth, because you have hidden these things from the wise and the intelligent and have revealed them to infants; yes, Father, for such was your gracious will" (Matthew 11:25–27; Luke 10:21).

Perhaps an announcement made by a five-year-old child in my early days in an atrium can expand my limited expectations. After presenting the account of Mary and Joseph fleeing to Egypt in order escape Herod's plan to kill all the babies, I asked the children, "I wonder what would have happened if Joseph had not listened to the angel in his dream?" Without hesitation this child responded, "The angel would keep coming back because God never gives up on us."

Perhaps the man in white represents us: those who proclaim the Gospel but are in need of forgiveness for deep-seated arrogance and limited vision. Perhaps the women represent children: those whose seemingly insignificant insights we often hurry by, those who are unafraid to approach the tomb because they need to be near their Lord and Savior, their Good Shepherd alive and active in their lives.

CHAPTER TWENTY

A Serious Love

Three children stood before the glass bowl of water on the low table. On one side of the table sat a large, rambling vine and on the other side, the Bible. As one child splashed water on another child's hands, the third child read from Psalm 51: "Create in [the child's name] a clean heart, O God; and put a right spirit within [him/her]." Then the children changed places and repeated the process. Groups of three came forward until all had a chance to participate. These children had already spent four weeks contemplating the parable of the True Vine; and the hand washing ceremony, better known as a communal celebration of reconciliation, took place during their solemn or first communion retreat.

Although I had planned this ceremony myself, I only became fully aware of its essence as I watched the children pray solemnly for each other. In fact, when asked earlier what kind of love God, the Vinedresser, has for us, they responded with "serious, a serious love." Once again, the children upset my boatload of assumptions about children and their capacity to know and name divine life and love. After twenty years in this work, I still need reminding that children are precious pearls in our midst, leaven lifting the rest of us up to greater consciousness; they are hidden treasures in the great field of the Church.

The serious love of God is "a love that does not rest," explained one child. It is a love on the move: searching, transforming, naming, encouraging, and celebrating our collaboration in God's plan for communion among all peoples and all creation. The parable of the True Vine, like the parables of the Kingdom of God, makes a bold statement, a serious and solid announcement of God's dependability. In it, Jesus states clearly who God is and who we are. "I am the true vine and my Father is the vinegrower . . . you are the branches" (John 15:1, 5). Jesus does not say, "I hope/want/should/plan to be the true vine," but "I am." I am the one in whom you "live and move and have [your] being" (Acts 17:28). It is a serious announcement but also one replete with dignity.

God's serious love waits for our response. Christ the True Vine waits for us to realize and rejoice in his invitation to "Abide in me as I abide in you" (see John 15:4–9). With the children we wonder: What does it mean to abide or to remain? What could Jesus be hoping for? How does a branch abide on a living vine? What is necessary for abiding? Does it take effort? I wonder what Jesus is trying to communicate when he says, "I am the Vine and you are the branches" (John 15:1)?

This is the way of parables. In parables we come as close as we possibly can to the mind of God. The Catechesis of the Good Shepherd is initiation into the parable method, into the way Jesus revealed divine life and love. In fact, before it was called the Catechesis of the Good Shepherd, this approach to children's religious formation was simply called the parable method. Both Maria Montessori and Sofia Cavalletti felt a strong need to return to scripture-based catechesis. Formalistic and definition-based curricula rob people of the joy of discovering they are the sheep of the Good Shepherd and the branches on the True Vine. They are the ones Jesus knows and calls by name. They are the ones invited to abide in him, to rest in his loving presence.

Cavalletti insists that the method used to communicate the mystery of God and God's kingdom must match the content. The mystery of God is so great a mystery that it cannot be contained in a single word, image, or definition. Jesus makes this clear when he offers numerous parables of the kingdom of God as well as different images of himself: the Light of the World; the Bread of Life; the way, the truth and the life; the Resurrection and the life. The serious love of God of which the children spoke is a love that allows for our prolonged meditation, for our gradual discovery that we are worthy of living near to God. We are worthy of being Christ's branches. We are worthy of receiving the life of God that runs through all the branches on the Vine.

Lent, then, is a period of time for taking God's infinite love seriously. It is a time for remaining—for remembering, returning, and renaming our life with God and with one another. It is a time for washing one another's hands and feet, hearts and wounds, for praying for one another, and for waiting patiently for the leaven to rise and the treasure in us to be revealed. It is a time for watching as the Vinedresser's serious love enfolds us again and again, but probably not as we imagine.

CHAPTER TWENTY-ONE

A Tender Caress

On the Friday before Holy Week a small group of families had gathered to walk through and pray a simple, experiential Stations of the Cross written by a friend of mine. It consisted of a brief Scripture text, an accompanying prayer, and a simple activity at each station. The activities were things like carrying a large wooden cross from one side of the church to the other, tasting vinegar, dabbing one another's faces with a moist cloth, and holding the eighteen-inch crucifix that usually hangs on the church wall near the pulpit. The activity of holding the crucifix corresponded to the station where Simon helps Jesus carrying the cross. The instructions read: "Pick up the crucifix and touch it any way you like." Slowing, a six-year-old child picked up the crucifix and, reverently cradling it in her arms like a baby doll, stroked the figure of Jesus for what seemed like an eternity. It seemed like time stopped as we all watched, captivated. None of us had ever seen such a gesture, such a tender caress of Jesus on the cross. The rest of the children followed this first child's lead. So did the adults.

Writing about this moment almost seems disrespectful. It was so intimate, so holy, and so powerful. Putting it in the public eye seems akin to photographing someone in prayer. Years earlier I fought to keep photographing children at work in the atrium to a bare minimum. The atrium is a place of prayer where work becomes conversation with God. Photographing anyone in prayer is intrusive, but it is especially so with regard to children who quickly hide their sacred side when adults show disrespect.

I close with this astonishing moment only to highlight how much children can teach us if we allow space for their own authentic responses. At the same time, we must also be intentional in listening to the child's ways of knowing and loving God in Christ the Good Shepherd. It is like listening to the wind in the trees, the gurgling of the river, or the song of a bird. "They will awaken something within the heart that is beyond all knowledge. Such is the teaching of the child. Yet the wind has the capacity to dig through rock and give rise to the movement of oceans."[1]

Watching this child tenderly caress Jesus on the cross was indeed a moment when the wind quietly shaved a huge chunk from the hardness of my own preconceived assumptions about children and about proper veneration of the cross. "Indeed, there are many sounds in the world; thus it is necessary for us to be very vigilant if we are to discern the sound God makes, at times barely perceptible, when speaking through his smallest creatures." May we all be vigilant advocates for children and their spiritual lives.

1　Anthony DeMello. *The Song of the Bird* (New York: Image Books, Doubleday, 1982), quoted in Sofia Cavalletti, "The Royal Road of Holy Joy," *The Journal of the Catechesis of the Good Shepherd* 17 (2002): 8–11.

ACKNOWLEDGMENTS

There are so many people who have brought me to this place of writing this book I scarcely know where to begin giving thanks, so I'll just begin at the beginning with my parents Bill and Martha Buchert for their example of faithfulness to God and the Church. Next, I am deeply grateful for the companionship and patience of my first formation leaders: Tina Lillig and Carol Nyberg. They were the first ones to help me fall in love with the Good Shepherd, the atrium, the children, and the families with whom I have had the honor of sharing the Catechesis of the Good Shepherd. Tina, thank you for paving the way and encouraging me to compile my twenty years of parish newsletter articles into this book.

I extend a huge thank you to my catechist buddies throughout the U.S. and beyond. What a gift it is to be bound together by this work of listening to God with children.

The Chicago area catechists are particularly precious to me. Thank you for your friendship, support, faith, humor, and especially your love. I could never have done it without you cheering me on: Suzanne Haraburd, Nerissa Breckbauer, Carol Cade, Betsy Peterson, Joan Roberts, and Harriet Claiborne.

I am greatly indebted to my friends outside the CGS community, especially Coni Sharp, Carole LoGalbo, and Eileen Peterson who have let me ramble on for hours about the atrium experience. Thank you for your gentle guidance and insights.

Many thanks to the clergy who have understood my vocation as a catechist and let me run wild with it: John McCausland and Jane Henderson.

To my editors at LTP, Margaret Brennan and Nora Malone, thank you for making the publishing process a complete joy. Your gracious and generous spirits will remain with me always.

Last and most important of all, I give thanks for my husband John and our girls, Amy, Terri, and Lisa. Even though it may have appeared at times that the Catechesis of the Good Shepherd is the most important thing to me, the truth is that you are my most precious pearls.

BIBLIOGRAPHY

Catechesis of the Good Shepherd National Office. www.cgsusa. org. Introductory brochure.

Cavalletti, Sofia. *History's Golden Thread.* Chicago: Liturgy Training Publications, 1999.

_____ *The Religious Potential of the Child.* Chicago: Liturgy Training Publications, 1992.

_____ *The Religious Potential of the Child 6 to 12 Years Old.* Chicago: Liturgy Training Publications, 2002.

_____ "The Royal Road of Holy Joy." *The Catechesis of the Good Shepherd Journal* 17 (2002): 8-11.

Cocchini, Tilde. "Artistic Expression of Children in the Atrium." *The Catechesis of the Good Shepherd Journal* 16 (2001): 14–17.

Coles, Robert. *The Spiritual Life of Children.* Boston, MA: Houghton Mifflin Co., 1990.

Devries, Dawn. "Toward a Theology of Childhood." *Interpretation* 55, no. 2 (April 2001).

Greenleaf, Robert. *Servant Leadership.* New York: Paulist Press, 1977.

Gobbi, Gianna. *Listening to God with Children.* Loveland, OH: Treehaus Communications, Inc., 1998.

Hooker, Morna D. *Jesus and the Servant*. London: S.P.C.K., 1959.

Jaworski, Joseph. *Synchronicity: The Inner Path of Leadership*. San Franscisco: Berrett-Koehler, 1998.

Montessori, Maria. *The Child in the Church*. St. Paul, MN: North Central Publishing Co., 1965.

Pritchard, Gretchen Wolff. *Offering the Gospel to Children*. Cambridge, MA: Cowley Publications, 1992.

The Book of Common Prayer for the Episcopal Church. New York: Oxford University Press, 1990.

The Roman Missal. Washington, DC: International Commission on English in the Liturgy, Inc., 2010.

Ulich, Robert. *A History of Religious Education: Documents and Interpretations from the Judaeo-Christian Tradition*. New York: New York University Press, 1968.